19.50

Virginia

By Jan Mader

Consultant
Nanci R. Vargus, Ed.D.
Primary Multiage Teacher
Decatur Township Schools, Indianapolis, Indiana

Children's Press®
A Division of Scholastic Inc.
New York   Toronto   London   Auckland   Sydney
Mexico City   New Delhi   Hong Kong
Danbury, Connecticut

Designer: Herman Adler Design
Photo Researcher: Caroline Anderson
The photo on the cover shows the Peaks of Otter, Blue Ridge Parkway.

Library of Congress Cataloging-in-Publication Data

Mader, Jan.
  Virginia / by Jan Mader.
      p. cm. — (Rookie read-about geography)
Includes index.
Summary: A simple introduction to Virginia, focusing on its geographical
features and points of interest.
  ISBN 0-516-22718-1 (lib. bdg.)   0-516-27780-4 (pbk.)
  1. Virginia—Juvenile literature. 2. Virginia—Geography—Juvenile
literature. [1. Virginia.] I. Title. II. Series.
  F226.3 .M33 2003
  917.55—dc21

                                    2002011563

1 2 3 4 5 6 7 8 9 10 R 12 11 10 09 08 07 06 05 04 03

Which state gave us
eight presidents?

The state of Virginia!

Eight presidents came from Virginia. Two of them were George Washington and Thomas Jefferson.

George Washington

Thomas Jefferson

6

The land in Virginia is
not the same everywhere.
There are mountains, hills,
and flat land, too.

The Appalachian (a-puh-
LAY-shee-uhn) Mountains
are in Western Virginia.
The Blue Ridge Mountains
are also there.

The middle of Virginia is called the Piedmont (PEED-mahnt). Piedmont is a French word. It means "at the foot of the mountains."

The Piedmont is hilly. Many large rivers flow across it.

10

Eastern Virginia is a coastal plain. This means the land is low and flat near the ocean. This part of Virginia is sometimes called the Tidewater.

Do you see the Chesapeake (CHEH-suh-peek) Bay on this map?

Water from the Atlantic Ocean flows into this bay. A bay is a part of the ocean that has some land around it.

North
West ✦ East
South

OHIO

PENNSYLVANIA

MARYLAND

DELAWARE

WEST
VIRGINIA

Blue Ridge Mountains

KENTUCKY

Richmond ★

Assateague
Island

Chesapeake Bay

VIRGINIA

TENNESSEE

SCALE 1 inch = 100 miles

0   Miles   100

0   Kilometers   160

NORTH CAROLINA

13

Across the bay is Virginia's Eastern Shore. There are many swamps and islands (EYE-luhndz) there.

Assateague (AS-uh-teeg) Island is famous for its wild ponies.

Virginia has many forests.
Black bears can be found
in the wooded mountains
and swamps.

Deer and foxes live
in the woods, too.

Virginia is warm most of the time. The temperature (TEM-pur-uh-chur) can reach 50 degrees Fahrenheit (FA-ren-hite) in February.

In the summer, the temperature can be hotter than 90 degrees Fahrenheit.

Virginia is beautiful in the fall. Many people visit Virginia to see the colorful trees.

Spring in Virginia is a time
for flowers, butterflies,
and birds. The cardinal is
the state bird.

People in Virginia do many
kinds of work. They work
in hospitals and offices.

Some people work in
coal mines.

Some people in Virginia are farmers. They grow tobacco, apples, and corn.

Other people fish. They
catch oysters and crabs.

Visitors to Virginia enjoy Williamsburg and Jamestown. These villages look like they did in the 1700s. The guides are dressed in costumes.

Virginia Beach is another great place to visit. People come from all over the world to have fun there.

Words You Know

black bear

Blue Ridge Mountains

cardinal

30

wild ponies

Williamsburg

Virginia Beach

31

Index

About the Author

Jan Mader has been writing for children for 15 years. Her natural curiosity and joy of life characterize her work in more than 24 published easy-reader stories.

Photo Credits

Photographs © 2003: Corbis Images/The Purcell Team: 18; Dembinsky Photo Assoc./Bill Lea: 16, 30 top left; Folio, Inc.: 20 (Ted Hooper), 27 right, 27 left, 31 bottom left (Richard T. Nowitz); H. Armstrong Roberts, Inc.: cover (T. Algire), 28, 31 bottom right (J. Blank), 15, 31 top (E.R. Degginger); Peter Arnold Inc./S.J. Krasemann: 21, 30 bottom; Photri Inc.: 5 bottom (Microstock), 24 (Richard T. Nowitz), 17 (Ann & Rob Simpson), 5 top, 9; Portfolio Group/Carl Purcell: 29; Stock Boston: 6, 30 top right (Thomas R. Fletcher), 23 (Owen Franken); The Image Works/Sonda Dawes: 22, 25; Unicorn Stock Photos/Ann & Rob Simpson: 10, 14.

Maps by Bob Italiano